# A Queer

# Theory

# of the State

## Samuel

## Clowes Huneke

*A Queer Theory of the State* is the sixth installment of the Critic's Essay Series published by Floating Opera Press. Comprising long-form essays, the series gives voice to critics who offer thought-provoking ways in which to subvert or replace normative modes of discussing culture and the world beyond.

For Paul Robinson

# Contents

It is one life in all, a grand object, a great purpose and content on which depend all individual happiness and all private decisions.
— G.W. F. Hegel, *Reason in History*

# Introduction

Disease has a way of clarifying things. Back in July 2022, I was running late, and I was panicking. On my way to get the first dose of Jynneos, the smallpox vaccine that also protects against mpox, I realized that, because of a snafu involving calendars and time zones, I was going to be over an hour late. The disease had started spreading rapidly among queer people in Western Europe and the United States, causing extremely painful symptoms. And despite ample warning and a good understanding of the virus, the United States government had been distressingly lackadaisical in its rollout of the vaccine. I was terrified that, if I missed my appointment, they would give away my dose and I wouldn't be able to reschedule for weeks, or even months. A sickening sense of déjà vu spread throughout my body, a visceral reminder of the rush to get COVID-19 vaccines only a year before. Luckily, the nurses didn't bat an eye at my tardiness. I got the vaccine and, a few weeks later, the second shot. After several anxious months, my life returned to normal—whatever that is.

The mpox scare of 2022, which may have passed most straight Americans by, turned into a queer movement in miniature, so to speak, that summer. Gay men were particularly at risk of the disease, which, although not an STI, seemed to be spreading primarily through sexual contact. It caused fever, lesions, hives, and such intense pain while defecating that one patient reported, "I would literally scream out loud when I went to the bathroom."[1] Another described "excruciating pain—the worst pain of my life."[2] With a series of baffling missteps from President Joe Biden's administration—waiting to order vaccines, allowing them to expire, and refusing for far too long to specify who was most at risk—LGBTQ people grew alarmed, then restless, then angry. Those months were a scary time, as disinformation spread online and conservatives advocated forcibly quarantining queer people in camps.[3] For many, the slow government response signaled that the LGBTQ community had once again been abandoned, reminding many of the AIDS epidemic that began in the 1980s. My friend and colleague Jonathon Catlin became a literal poster boy for the protests,

Thousands of protesters march down Pennsylvania Avenue during the Women's March on Washington, DC, on January 21, 2017

holding a sign at a rally in July 2022 that asked, "Monkey-pox: Where Is Your RAGE?"[4] His photograph went viral, showing up everywhere from *Le Monde* to *Al Jazeera*.

It was an intentional sign, an allusion to radical AIDS activism from the 1980s. And he was hardly the only one to make the connection. In those months, the media was flooded with comparisons between mpox and HIV, with many insisting that these were similar crises: a virus spreading rapidly among queer men and a negligent government response. Others countered that they could not have been further apart. After all, the Biden administration, despite its lethargy, did eventually act to halt the disease's spread. And while mpox is intensely painful, it is not the death sentence that HIV once was. In a sense, then, the mpox summer became a kind of Rorschach test for LGBTQ activists and intellectuals steeped in queer theory. Where some saw the malevolence of the modern state and contemporary society, others saw an ultimately successful state intervention in public health that resolved the crisis within the span of a year.[5] It was a striking divergence in perspective, which pointed to deeper divisions within the queer community.

I was particularly struck by this divergence because it underscored a broader problem within queer theory, an academic field that continues to inform and be informed by LGBTQ activism. Queer scholarship and the deconstructionist philosophy from which it grew are recognized for their trenchant capacity to critique. By questioning everything from human intention to the very language we use, its practitioners are able to cut through the blandness of the everyday in order to understand what is really going on. It is a powerful tool to unearth the hidden norms that structure—and impoverish—our lives. In the case of mpox, activists leveraged its insights to highlight how structural inequities and prejudices had allowed the disease to spread and slowed the government's response.

At the same time, however, a relentless focus on critique hampers its ability to offer anything resembling solutions. The pages of queer theory abound with references to the "urgent work" of "coalition building" or "oppositional politics," but rarely offer anything resembling concrete proposals of what that really *means* or might actually look like. Much of queer theory suffers, that is, from an inability to think constructively, hamstrung by reflexive critique. It is a problem I've become increasingly troubled by, precisely because of how much I owe to the field, both as a gay man and as a queer intellectual.

I can still recall the visceral thrill of reading Michel Foucault's *The History of Sexuality* for the first time when I was twenty-two. I raced through it in a single afternoon while sitting at a sun-soaked table outside a third-wave coffee shop (and no, I was not eating avocado toast). As a college senior, I researched queer literature, discovering

Jonathon Catlin at an mpox protest in New York on July 21, 2022

AIDS Coalition to Unleash Power (ACT UP) activists holding posters asking "AIDS: Where is your rage?" in 1994

ancestors I never knew I had. These texts, which were part of my own coming out and coming to terms with my sexuality, offered a way of looking at the world beyond the humdrum of daily life. Much of that thrill was indeed found in critique, in tearing down totems of established thought. At the time, when I was young, I wasn't worried about what might replace that status quo. But by last summer—whether it's because I'm older, or because of all that has transpired over the last few years, or because I just really wanted that mpox vaccine—I was.

The source of this tension within queer studies, I've come to believe, lies in its inability to conceive positively of the state—that is, to explain what the state is (or ought to be) and why it should exist. It is a problem that stretches back to queer theory's origins and that we can only really begin to understand by asking what, precisely, "queer" is.

Once a slur, today it is a convenient shorthand to refer to lesbian, gay, bisexual, trans, and other sexually and gender-nonconforming people. It also carries political valences; those who identify as queer typically align with radical or progressive movements. Then there's academic queerness—a range of humanistic fields from queer theory to gender studies to the history of sexuality. For these thinkers, among whom I count myself, queer denotes a set of methodological approaches to the study of sex, gender, and sexuality—and their co-constitution with race, class, and ability—shaped by the work of deconstructionist philosophers in the second half of the twentieth century, including Jacques Derrida, Gilles Deleuze, and, most significantly, Foucault.

Foucault was, above all else, a theorist of power, by which he meant not the hierarchical domination exercised by governments, but rather the normative expectations that shape our lives. His works interrogated the "capillary functioning" of this form of power, which, he argued, had emerged in the modern period through everyday interactions and social institutions, from prisons to schools to clinics.[6] That conception of power was revolutionary, for it turned on its head the common sense of what was "normal," insisting that what we assume to be typical is, in fact, nothing more than a set of social constructs designed to control us.

In Foucault's understanding of modern society, Wendy Brown argues, "The state is not the wellspring or agent of all governing power, nor does it monopolize political power."[7] In this way, he and his heirs decentered the state, pleading for a political science that would "cut off the head of the king," as he so memorably put it.[8] Later scholarship on sexuality and gender took up the call to arms, focusing on the emergence of "normality" through modern medicine, universal schooling, the empirical sciences, and other institutions of social regulation. Here lay true power. The idea of a "power, construed as a subject, that acts," Judith Butler asserted in 1993, is nothing more than a myth. Rather, it was the "reiterated acting" of daily life that "*is* power."[9] Human agency is—largely—a fiction, the state and high politics mere expressions of deeper power relations, which emerge from language and culture.

These were profoundly generative ideas at the time, not only to scholars like Butler, Eve Kosofsky Sedgwick, Lauren Berlant, and Michael Warner, but also to queer liberation groups of the 1980s and 1990s. A generation of historians, many of them activists, began to unearth how the persecution of queer people had shifted over time, revealing that it was not historically inevitable.[10] These efforts—what we might think of as the queer political project—were thus aimed at the deconstruction of norms and the consequent proliferation of life opportunities in the modern world. By exposing normality as nothing more than a fiction wormed into our very sense of self—and by transforming this realization into activist imperative—queer studies became a field that was, in the words of David Halperin, "at odds with the normal, the legitimate, the dominant."[11]

Hence, queerness and the state were doubly alienated. Not only did queer theory have little interest in the state, it also had no use for it. After all, the state is, in itself, that which is normal, legitimate, and dominant.

1    Sebastian Köhn and Wilfred Chan, "'I Literally Screamed Out Loud in Pain': My Two Weeks of Monkeypox Hell," *The Guardian*, July 23, 2022, https://www.theguardian.com/world/2022/jul/23/i-literally-screamed-out-loud-in-pain-my-two-weeks-of-monkeypox-hell.

2    Jamie Ducharme, Angela Haupt, and Jeffrey Kluger, "What It Really Feels Like to Have Monkeypox," *Time*, August 1, 2022, https://time.com/6201191/what-monkeypox-feels-like/.

3    Trudy Ring, "Right-Winger Calls for LGBTQ+ People to Be Put in Camps Over Monkeypox," *Advocate*, August 6, 2022, https://www.advocate.com/news/2022/8/06/right-winger-calls-lgbtq-people-be-put-camps-over-monkeypox.

4    Jonathon Catlin, "I Became the Poster Boy for Monkeypox Activism, But There's Much More to This Story," *Huffington Post*, August 6, 2022, https://www.huffpost.com/entry/monkeypox-vaccines-covid-aids-activism_n_62ea9bebe4b00f4cf2369bea.

5    Alex Abad-Santos, "The US Monkeypox Response Is Failing Queer Men," *Vox*, August 11, 2022, https://www.vox.com/culture/23292430/monkeypox-outbreak-us-gay-men; Fenit Nirappil, "How the Monkeypox Outbreak Revealed the Path for Vanquishing Viruses," *Washington Post*, 30 December 2022, https://www.washingtonpost.com/health/2022/12/30/monkeypox-how-to-defeat-virus/.

6    Michel Foucault, *Discipline and Punish: The Birth of the Prison*, trans. Alan Sheridan (New York: Vintage, 1995), 198.

7    Wendy Brown, *Regulating Aversion: Tolerance in the Age of Identity and Empire* (Princeton, NJ: Princeton University Press, 2008), 79.

8    Michel Foucault, *The History of Sexuality: An Introduction*, trans. Robert Hurley (New York: Vintage, 1990), 88–89; see also Stephen W. Sawyer, "Foucault and the State," *The Tocqueville Review* XXXVI, no. 1 (2015): 135–64.

9    Judith Butler, "Critically Queer," *GLQ* 1 (1993): 17.

10   Jim Downs, "The Education of Jonathan Ned Katz," *The Chronicle of Higher Education*, February 21, 2016, https://www.chronicle.com/article/the-education-of-jonathan-ned-katz.

11   David Halperin, *Saint Foucault: Towards a Gay Hagiography* (New York: Oxford University Press, 1995), 62.

# I
# Neoliberal Queers

In turning against the state, these thinkers were riding the cresting wave of history. From Roosevelt's New Deal of the 1930s, which sought to drag the country out of the Great Depression, to the USSR's Five-Year Plans to industrialize the national economy, faith in the state's awesome power had only grown in the middle of the twentieth century. But, by the 1970s—in the wake of the Vietnam War and successive revelations of Stalinist horrors—the endemic inefficiencies, petty corruptions, and coziness of government with corporations and labor unions alike began to alienate a new generation of leftists. Institutionally, these trends propelled a shift toward left neoliberalism in the 1990s, embodied in figures like Bill Clinton in the United States and Tony Blair in the United Kingdom, who rejected the class-based politics of the old left. In its place, they inaugurated a marriage of identity-based social liberalism and laissez-faire market reforms.[1]

Burgeoning queer movements in this period followed a similar trajectory. From the Gay Liberation Front—which grew out of the Stonewall riots of 1969—to STAR (Street Transvestite Action Revolutionaries) to ACT UP (AIDS Coalition to Unleash Power), Western queer movements turned to everyday modes of resistance and world building, repudiating the state-leaning approaches of older homophile movements. They pursued novel strategies and programs, from "zaps" (targeted disruptions designed to embarrass public figures) and sit-ins to providing housing and hospice care. In doing so, these groups often rejected the legitimacy and the efficacy of the state. They believed, in Michael Warner's words, "that political struggles were to be carried out neither through the normal state apparatus nor through revolutionary combat."[2] Imbued with a Foucauldian spirit, queerness, along with much of the contemporary left, turned slowly but surely away from the sociopolitical and toward the cultural realm, where activists believed true liberation might be found.[3]

In its early years, queer theory's shift toward language and culture as sites of power was thus predicated on a turn away from not just the state but also class. That is, whereas the "old left" and allied scholars had seen in class politics and socio-economic inquiry the path to

David Robinson, ACT UP founding member and Ashes Action organizer, Washington, DC, 1992

progress, queer theorists and the new left often preferred to talk about overlapping forms of identity or difference, most prominently race, gender, and sexuality. Precisely because queerness rarely spoke in terms of class, except through what Petrus Liu has called "a moralizing language against privilege or discrimination," some of its identity-based demands have been easily co-opted by the class-blind logics of neoliberalism.[4] It's an increasingly common critique: that by focusing on language, culture, and norms at the expense of law, politics, and class, queer theory not only indulged in what Martha McCluskey terms "queer anti-statism," but has even acted as a handmaid of neoliberal capitalism.[5] Ironically, of course, right-wing proponents of economic neoliberalism were just as often hostile to the kind of social liberalism that this critique associates with queer theory.[6]

Even in the 1990s—as the discipline of queer theory began to emerge from a heady concatenation of post-structuralist philosophy, the history of sexuality, and literary studies—rumblings of discontent could already be heard. In 1994, Lisa Duggan warned against the political quietism of queer critique. In a short essay on "queering the state," she skewered faux radicals who "presented as the progressive cutting edge of politics as well as theory," but who in truth were guilty of "avoiding (if not outright despising) lesbian/gay/queer activism."[7] She argued instead that politics could make use of the strategic insights queer theory had to offer. Acknowledging how queer theory had led many of its adherents to reject the mucky realities of politics, Duggan nonetheless insisted upon the continuing need for the state, asserting "this is not the historical moment when we want to set up a negative relation to state power or slip into limiting forms of libertarianism."[8]

Duggan was right. For if the decades-long experiment with neoliberalism has taught us anything, it is that we do need what Michael Walzer once called the "directing center."[9] Hollowed out by both liberal and conservative parties, many contemporary states have become unable to redistribute wealth, care for citizens, address climate change, or forge genuine social equality. If nothing else, massive, though flawed, government efforts to contain viruses from HIV to mpox to COVID-19 demonstrate the need for powerful states that can dictate public-health measures and compel citizens to behave in responsible ways.

Viewed from the perspective of queer people, the need for a muscular, progressive state is no less great. We want health services that offer gender-affirming care, do we not? We want a state that will provide universal childcare to ensure an ungendered division of labor. Surely, we hope for a state that will protect minorities from social discrimination and violence. It may not be sexy or edgy to admit, especially at a time when the radical right is turning to state power in service of its patriarchal social vision, but we queers do need the state.

The question, then, is whether it is possible to work out a theory of the state that unites the critically anti-normative impulses of queer theory and the empirical need for the state, coercive though it may be. While I am certainly not the first to grapple with these questions, much of what has been written on the subject falls into one of two camps: radicals who reject political compromise or pragmatists who begrudgingly embrace it. Neither has been able to give a positive account of state power, one that would legitimate its exercise in service of a twenty-first-century progressivism. We "know what is wrong with this world," to take Brown's words, "but cannot articulate a road out."[10] And while it may seem like an exercise in mere sophistry, I continue to believe it important for queer progressives to explain and defend a vision of the state. To put it in more personal terms: I, a scholar with an abiding commitment to queer theory, have long found myself unable to leverage its insights to explain why I also favor a powerful, progressive state.

Such a theory of the state, as I see it, would not only encompass government for self-identified queer people. This is no project of escapism, nor of ghettoization. Rather, it is about envisioning a state that best allows all people—whether cis, trans, nonbinary, gay, straight, lesbian, bi, or queer—to live to their fullest potential, free of stultifying norms and the excesses of capital. It is a difficult task, but the challenge is also an opportunity. For if there is any hope that progress will be more than an empty slogan for the sclerotic parties of the left, then it must be in a politics that takes seriously the kinds of violent marginalization and insidious norms that are the special preoccupations of queer studies, while at the same time offering a positive vision of state power.

1   Paul Sabin, *Public Citizens: The Attack on Big Government and the Remaking of American Liberalism* (New York: Norton, 2021); Nancy Fraser, "From Progressive Neoliberalism to Trump—and Beyond," *American Affairs* I, no. 4 (Winter 2017): 46–64.

2   Michael Warner, "Something Queer About the Nation-State," in *After Political Correctness: Humanities and Society in the 1990s*, ed. Christopher Newfield and Ronald Strickland (London: Routledge, 1995), 362.

3   William J. Novak and Stephen W. Sawyer, "Epilogue: The Need for a New and Critical Democracy," *The Tocqueville Review* XLI, no. 2 (2020): 110.

4   Petrus Liu, *The Specter of Materialism: Queer Theory and Marxism in the Age of the Beijing Consensus* (Durham, NC: Duke University Press, 2023), 22.

5   Martha T. McCluskey, "How Queer Theory Makes Neoliberalism Sexy," in *Feminist and Queer Legal Theory: Intimate Encounters, Uncomfortable Conversations*, ed. Martha Albertson Fineman, Jack E. Jackson, and Adam P. Romero (London: Routledge, 2009), 120.

6   Quinn Slobodian, *Globalists: The End of Empire and the Birth of Neoliberalism* (Cambridge, MA: Harvard University Press, 2018), 121–81.

7   Lisa Duggan, "Queering the State," *Social Text* 39 (Summer 1994): 5.

8   Duggan, "Queering the State," 11.

9   Michael Walzer, "The Politics of Michel Foucault," *Dissent* (Fall 1983), 483.

10  Wendy Brown, *Undoing the Demos: Neoliberalism's Stealth Revolution* (New York: Zone Books, 2015), 220.

# II
# Radical Utopias

None of this is to say that queerness is opposed to politics. Far from it. Most queer intellectuals see their work as deeply political, and queer texts have had a profound impact on activist movements that took up anti-normativity as a battle call. Especially in the United States—where the AIDS crisis of the 1980s and 1990s, intensified by the Reagan administration's willful neglect of victims, not only led to renewed LGBTQ activism but also shaped the emergence of queer theory—the fields of queer studies developed a particularly oppositional politics. As new queer activists mobilized against AIDS, queer theorists analyzed the strategies and the effects of their efforts. These groups were critical of pragmatic gay and lesbian efforts to work with the state, and for good reason: the president refused to so much as utter the word "AIDS" for four long years. ACT UP, which was founded in New York City in 1987, pioneered new direct-action strategies, such as die-ins and ashes actions, which drew attention to government neglect.

The radical utopianism that undergirded these efforts was founded on a profound distrust of the state, understanding it as an expression of deeper normative relations that constituted culture and society itself, relations that theorists contend are constitutionally hostile to LGBTQ people. This view drew on the Foucauldian canon, in particular the philosopher's dismissal of the state as "superstructural."[1] To change government policy, activists would have to change society, culture, and language itself. Not for nothing did David Halperin hear from ACT UP members that their "single most important intellectual source of political inspiration" was Foucault's *The History of Sexuality*.[2]

This activism's legacy lives on in queer theory through its dual critique of the state and embrace of a politics that prizes direct action and community organizing. In their 1995 essay "What Does Queer Theory Teach Us about X," Lauren Berlant and Michael Warner noted that "queer theory has flourished in the disciplines where expert service to the state has been least familiar."[3] Where queer theorists have addressed the state, it is usually to dismiss it as a locus of violence exercised against LGBTQ communities. The critic José Esteban Muñoz,

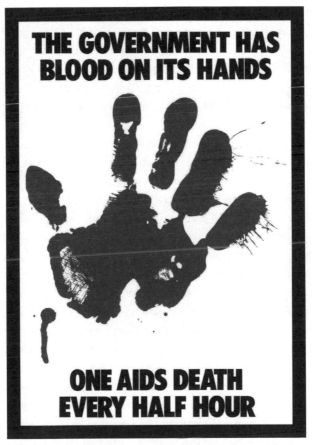

ACT UP activists pointed to the role that government neglect had played in allowing HIV to spread virtually unchecked in the United States. This poster was created by the artist collective Gran Fury, which was associated with ACT UP and is best known for its iconic "Silence = Death" poster.

for instance, described heteronormativity in his influential book *Cruising Utopia* as "the spectacle of the state refurbishing its ranks through overt and subsidized acts of reproduction."[4] In their recent monograph *Atmospheres of Violence*, Eric Stanley denounces "the state's violent expansion," arguing that "the state, even as an experiment in democracy, is unable to offer us relief."[5]

In many ways, this perspective echoes the concept of the state found in German thinker Walter Benjamin's critique of power (*Gewalt*—a capacious term that can also be translated as violence, force, or authority). Like Benjamin—who is among queer theory's favorite philosophers—scholars critique what he termed "law-preserving power," the pervasive "threatening" force that maintains the status quo. With this formulation, Benjamin contended that power sat at "the origin" of law itself, that no matter how it is dressed up, right is always the product of might. When a new form of power overwhelms the law-preserving force of the status quo, it can birth a new state, an exercise that Benjamin terms "law-creating power."[6] This dialectic of power, which he suggests undergirds modern societies, is then mythologized as a way of obscuring the paradox that all law—all state power—is fundamentally created and upheld by violence. This process of mythologization is similar, though not identical, to what Foucault meant by normative power. While the state's (theoretical) monopoly on the use of violent force provides an ultimate backstop, it is through the mythologies of daily life and bureaucratic practice that its power is most often exercised.

Queer theory has sought to expose this dialectic, pointing out the incipient insidiousness of modern systems of governance and demythologizing the violence that props up state power. Born of the critical impulses embodied within queerness, this line of thought has proven to be a potent way for the marginalized to diagnose the ills of the societies they inhabit. On occasion, it can also lead to paranoid thinking, such as those who interpreted government incompetence around mpox as incontrovertible evidence of deep-seated animus. And, more significantly, while these analyses are vitally important, few confront the question that invariably arises: What happens after you expose the violence of state power?

At first blush, it might seem that the answer lies in the realm of liberal political philosophy. After all, liberal thought, which began to cohere in the late eighteenth and early nineteenth centuries in the writings of Adam Smith, John Stuart Mill, and other Enlightenment philosophers, tends to view the state as a fundamental antagonist to liberty. "The fear and favor that have always inhibited freedom," the philosopher Judith N. Shklar wrote in 1989, "are overwhelmingly generated by governments."[7] When Ronald Reagan told voters that "the nine most terrifying words in the English language are:

I'm from the government, and I'm here to help,"[8] it was nothing more than a bowdlerized variation on a liberal theme that had been playing for over two centuries.

Taking the sovereign individual as its point of departure, liberalism seeks state—and market—forms that permit the greatest flexibility possible with minimum interference from the government. But while there has historically been considerable sympathy between liberal political movements and sexually marginalized groups, contemporary queer writings often reserve their harshest salvos for liberalism. Such analysis—much of which comes out of queer of color critique and its concern with racial capitalism—typically points to liberalism's ideological function as a handmaid of modern capital.[9] Liberalism's talk of individual rights and freedom of expression are taken as mere cover for the rapaciousness of an unregulated economy into which certain queer populations, such as white cisgender gay men, "have become absorbable" through what Kadji Amin calls "a neoliberal politics of lifestyle choice and anodyne diversity."[10] This is the kind of identity politics to which gay liberals like Andrew Sullivan subscribe, one that "focuses only on the relation between the state and individuals and rejects any state responsibility for the social status or welfare of citizens."[11] Thus, when LGBTQ movements have successfully made demands of the state—marriage equality, an end to "don't ask, don't tell"—queer critics have pointed, justifiably, to how those very policies further an assimilationist agenda, what Lisa Duggan criticized in 2002 as "homonormativity." Such policies shore up neo-liberal capitalism by substituting radical queer activism with "domesticated, depoliticized privacy" accessible only to certain classes of already-privileged queers.[12] The very "intelligibility" of identity on which such a politics rests—who will have access to these newly domesticated rights—therefore makes "racialized anti-trans/queer violence," as Eric Stanley argues, a "necessary expression of the liberal state."[13]

There is something inherently hypocritical about liberalism. Despite the fine, flowery language regarding rights on which it is predicated, the de facto exclusion of whole swathes of the population from those rights is left unsaid. The United States Declaration of Independence may have promised "life, liberty, and the pursuit of happiness" to all people, but at the time of its signing, hundreds of thousands of Black Americans were kept as enslaved laborers. The much-vaunted democracies of Western Europe long restricted the franchise to propertied men. The last European jurisdiction to grant universal suffrage, a small Swiss canton, only did so in 1990. And democracies have been among the most egregious violators of the human rights of sex- and gender-nonconforming people. From sodomy laws and sumptuary codes to homophobic asylum policies and the

United States prison-industrial complex, liberal states have proved themselves profoundly and hypocritically hostile to those on society's margins. By highlighting both the violence underpinning liberal forms of government and the institutionalized neglect of marginalized communities, queer scholarship has effectively put the lie to the (neo)liberal conceit that, as Henry David Thoreau framed it, "that government is best which governs least."[14]

Such critiques are nothing new. In 1984, Shklar, a liberal to be sure, but also one of liberalism's keenest critics, pointed out that "the revolt of private conscience against liberal governments" was due not "to their exceptional depravity, but to the extraordinary hopes that liberalism once inspired."[15] Queer thinkers—along with critical race theorists and feminist scholars—object not so much to the liberal tradition's universalizing claims as such, but rather to the regularity with which liberal states *fail to live up to* those claims.

Critique of liberalism can even shade into a skepticism toward democracy. Stanley, for one, decries "the celebration of unfreedom we call democracy."[16] C. Riley Snorton has argued—and not without cause—that "traditional notions of democracy" are "inextricably tied to national belonging, whiteness, and heteronormativity."[17] Likewise, in their last monograph, Berlant challenged the way that democratic decision-making provides cover for inequities in contemporary society.[18] Nor does the Foucauldian heritage offer a theory—let alone a defense— of democracy (in part because Foucault was little concerned with questions of political legitimacy).[19] Even where queer theorists embrace the term, they often do so as a social process, as "democratization" rather than "democracy."[20] But queer reservations about democracy's majoritarian underpinnings are nothing new, and they come from a long history of persecution at the hands of hypocritical democratic governments.[21]

While Shklar—who made a career excavating liberalism's emotional underbelly—recognized the powerful role that anti-hypocrisy plays in modern politics, she also insisted that it was a profoundly unstable basis on which to build a theory of state. Although hatred of hypocrisy might be "a splendid weapon of psychic warfare," in her formulation (and it is indeed a potent tool of queer politics—pointing out the gap between politicians' words and deeds), it also enshrines an unattainable moral absolute as the standard of good policy, thereby excluding the very messiness of politics.[22] Anti-hypocrisy can quickly curdle into cruelty, an utter intolerance for that with which you disagree. Read through Shklar's diagnosis of an anti-hypocritical politics, it becomes clear why queer theory, while proclaiming its own anti-normativity, so often seems to be driven by a set of rigidly applied norms and why its authors so often sink into cynicism. In its critique of liberalism, queer theory returns to square one when it comes to the state. A liberal state is at once too large and too small, hypocritically offering cover for laissez-faire neoliberalism while failing to protect those most in need.

In response to the mounting disenchantment with liberal democracy, a number of theorists have offered queer Marxism as a solution. If queer Marxism sounds like a paradox or the butt of a joke, that's because, for a long time, it was. Queer theory's rejection of class politics and the state had long provoked overhyped charges from the Marxian left that queerness was actively complicit in the neoliberal dismantling of the welfare state. In turn, queer scholars have pointed to how socialists from Marx onward routinely ignored or even persecuted LGBTQ people.[23]

Queer Marxists writing today do not so much deny this fraught history as they seek to demonstrate how the interests of queer people and the working classes ought to intersect. Liu, for instance, has sought to resurrect queer traditions from early socialist China, while the late scholar Christopher Chitty argued that it was precisely at crises of early capitalism that queer subcultures formed and faced persecution.[24] Numerous other scholars have unearthed the considerable overlap among twentieth-century leftist and queer movements, highlighting that, in fact, the recent, assimilationist priorities of the LGBTQ movement obscure a longer history of class-based, queer radicalism.[25]

While these efforts offer an important mechanism to bridge the gap between different leftist idioms, they fail to resolve the problem of the state. Most of these works, embedded as they are within the assumptions and vernaculars of queer theory, tend to ignore the state or what role it might play in a queer Marxist world. Indeed, they often sidestep the problem of state form entirely, leaving open the fraught question of just what flavor of socialism a queer movement might advocate. Contemporary works of queer Marxism thus tend to offer at best a kind of left anarchist reading of queer theory, a way of unifying class- and identity-based approaches, but without suggesting concrete political action.

What remains, then, is the persistent question of how queer theory might contribute a positive vision of the state, its duties, and its prerogatives. Many get around the problem by simply ignoring it, implying that it might be better to do away with the state entirely. And they are not alone in this position. The works of anarchist scholars like James C. Scott and the late anthropologist David Graeber have enjoyed much attention in recent years as well as praise from queer scholars.[26] Ironically, many queer theorists, even as they demand greater protection and services from the state, often wind up sounding a great deal like left libertarians, yearning for

In the postwar period, queer activists across Western Europe and the United States often saw their goals aligned with socialism. Here, the sociologist and activist Martin Dannecker marches in the West German city of Münster with a sign proclaiming, "Brothers and sisters, whether gay or not, to fight capitalism is our lot!"

a world free of the state and its institutions. Berlant, for instance, opines that "institutions narrow access" to public goods.[27] It is a common conceit of queer theory that "access" somehow exists free of context, that it is, in fact, not institutions that *create*—however imperfectly—the very public goods to which we desire access. This conceit sits at the core of the anarcho-libertarian tendency that runs through queer theory: the utopian promise of doing away entirely with stultifying institutions. And it is no accident that these works also often reject the demands of empiricism.[28] Such language has become particularly pronounced in queer writings since the 2009 publication of *Cruising Utopia*, in which Muñoz poetically defines queer as "the warm illumination of a horizon imbued with potentiality" coupled with "the rejection of a here and now" and a "refusal of empiricist historiography."[29]

Of course, there is nothing so very novel about wanting to do away with the state: utopian and eschatological visions from *The Book of Revelation* to *The Communist Manifesto* have prophesied an end to temporal government. But it remains difficult to see how dire social, economic, and environmental problems will ever be addressed, let alone solved, without large-scale collective action, which is hard to imagine without the coercive power of the state. The direct action and community-building that queer theory so often proposes has historically been successful up to a point, but past that point has often

41

required (or even demanded) state interventions. Radical queer thought thus offers necessary critiques of all that is amiss with the mode of collective action we call the state but remains at best agnostic and at worst openly hostile to it. Instead, it cements a paradox: a boundless faith in the utopian horizon of queerness yoked to an absolute rejection of humans' capacity to govern themselves.

1 Michel Foucault, "Truth and Power," in Michel Foucault, *Knowledge-Power: Selected Interviews & Other Writings, 1972–1977*, ed. Colin Gordon (New York: Pantheon Books, 1980), 122.

2 David Halperin, *Saint Foucault: Towards a Gay Hagiography* (New York: Oxford University Press, 1995), 15.

3 Lauren Berlant and Michael Warner, "What Does Queer Theory Teach Us About X," *PMLA* 110, no. 3 (1995): 348.

4 José Esteban Muñoz, *Cruising Utopia: The Then and There of Queer Futurity* (New York: New York University Press, 2009), 22.

5 Eric Stanley, *Atmospheres of Violence: Structuring Antagonism and the Trans/Queer Ungovernable* (Durham, NC: Duke University Press, 2021), 5, 11.

6 Walter Benjamin, "Zur Kritik der Gewalt," in *Walter Benjamin, Gesammelte Schriften*, vol. II–I, ed. Rolf Tiedemann and Hermann Schweppenhäuser (Frankfurt: Suhrkamp, 1977), 188. Unless otherwise noted, all translations are my own.

7 Judith Shklar, "The Liberalism of Fear," in *Liberalism and the Moral Life*, ed. Nancy Rosenblum (Cambridge, MA: Harvard University Press, 1989), 21.

8 "August 12, 1986, Reagan Quotes and Speeches: News Conference—I'm here to help," *Ronald Reagan Presidential Foundation & Institute*, https://www.reaganfoundation.org/ronald-reagan/reagan-quotes-speeches/news-conference-1/.

9 See Roderick Ferguson, *Aberrations in Black: Toward a Queer of Color Critique* (Minneapolis, MN: University of Minnesota Press, 2004); Chandan Reddy, *Freedom With Violence: Race, Sexuality, and the US State* (Durham, NC: Duke University Press, 2011); and Grace Kyungwon Hong, *The Ruptures of American Capital: Women of Color Feminism and the Culture of Immigrant Labor* (Minneapolis, MN: University of Minnesota Press, 2006).

10 Kadji Amin, "Haunted by the 1990s: Queer Theory's Affective Histories," *Women's Studies Quarterly* 44, nos. 3/4 (Fall/Winter 2016): 183; see also Jennifer V. Evans, *The Queer Art of History: Queer Kinship after Fascism* (Durham, NC: Duke University Press, 2023), 5.

11 Shane Phelan, "Queer Liberalism?" *The American Politics Science Review* 94, no. 2 (June 2000): 432.

12 Lisa Duggan, "The New Homonormativity," in *Materializing Democracy: Toward a Revitalized Cultural Politics*, ed. Russ Castronovo and Dana D. Nelson (Durham, NC: Duke University Press, 2002), 190.

13 Stanley, *Atmospheres of Violence*, 10.

14  Henry David Thoreau, *On the Duty of Civil Disobedience* (London: Simple Life Press, 1903), 7.

15  Judith N. Shklar, *Ordinary Vices* (Cambridge, MA: Belknap Press, 1984), 67.

16  Stanley, *Atmospheres of Violence*, 10.

17  C. Riley Snorton, *Nobody Is Supposed to Know: Black Sexuality on the Down Low* (Minneapolis, MN: University of Minnesota Press, 2014), 29.

18  Lauren Berlant, *On the Inconvenience of Other People* (Durham, NC: Duke University Press, 2022), 11.

19  Wendy Brown, *Regulating Aversion: Tolerance in the Age of Identity and Empire* (Princeton, NJ: Princeton University Press, 2008), 83.

20  Judith Butler, "Critically Queer," *GLQ* 1 (1993): 19.

21  See Samuel Clowes Huneke, "Can Democracy be Queer? Male Homosexuality, Democratisation and the Law in Postwar Germany," *Contemporary European History* (2022): 1–13.

22  Shklar, *Ordinary Vices*, 69.

23  Mitchell Dean and Daniel Zamora, *The Last Man Takes LSD: Foucault and the End of Revolution* (London: Verso, 2021), 188; James Penney, *After Queer Theory: The Limits of Sexual Politics* (London: Pluto Press, 2014), 70–110.

24  Christopher Chitty, *Sexual Hegemony: Statecraft, Sodomy, and Capital in the Rise of the World System* (Durham, NC: Duke University Press, 2020); Petrus Liu, *The Specter of Materialism: Queer Theory and Marxism in the Age of the Beijing Consensus* (Durham, NC: Duke University Press, 2023), 81–103.

25  Aaron Lecklider, *Love's Next Meeting: The Forgotten History of Homosexuality and the Left in American Culture* (Berkeley: University of California Press, 2021); Samuel Clowes Huneke, *States of Liberation: Gay Men between Dictatorship and Democracy in Cold War Germany* (Toronto: University of Toronto Press, 2022).

26  David Graeber and David Wengrow, *The Dawn of Everything: A New History of Humanity* (New York: Farrar, Straus and Giroux, 2021); James C. Scott, *The Art of Not Being Governed: An Anarchist History of Upland Southeast Asia* (New Haven, CT: Yale University Press, 2009); Lauren Berlant, *Cruel Optimism* (Durham, NC: Duke University Press, 2011), 260; Jack Halberstam, *The Queer Art of Failure* (Durham, NC: Duke University Press, 2011), 9.

27  Berlant, *On the Inconvenience of Other People*, 78.

28  Heather Love, *Underdogs: Social Deviance and Queer Theory* (Chicago: University of Chicago Press, 2021), 146–49.

29  Muñoz, *Cruising Utopia*, 1, 17.

# III
# Queer Pragmatism

Much of the radical utopian tradition stems from the American academy and the experiences of queer people in the United States, shaped by the AIDS epidemic and marriage-equality debates. As I have grown as a queer scholar, though, I've approached many of these texts slant-wise, largely because my training is in German history—a more intellectually conservative field, to be sure, but also one rooted in a very different national experience. As a result, I am somewhat more sympathetic to a second strand of thought that dates back to the earliest queer political movements of nineteenth-century Europe. This tradition is best described as pragmatic and has, in recent years, received renewed attention from historians of sexuality.

How historians view the first homosexual rights movement, which evolved in Germany between the late nineteenth century and the Nazi takeover in 1933, provides a good example of the pragmatic tendency. Magnus Hirschfeld, the Weimar-era doctor and a leading figure in this movement, is still revered for his enterprising work in sexology and for his pioneering activism, with several national organizations in Germany bearing his name. Yet, in recent years he has come under increasing critical scrutiny for his prioritization of incremental reform, his fraught relationship with colonialism, and his racist language.[1]

These critiques, however, have not led to a wholesale repudiation of the man or the movement for gay rights that he represented. Rather, as German studies scholar Javier Samper Vendrell argues, a careful balancing act between radical aspirations and pragmatic necessities shaped homosexual rights activism in the Weimar Republic. Even while critiquing the man and the politics he represents, historians continue to appreciate the clarity with which he fought for queer rights, understanding his efforts as an important prefiguration of later, more radical movements.[2] Unlike more utopian views of queerness, such approaches center what historian Craig Griffiths has termed "the ambivalence of gay liberation."[3] In doing so, they do not attempt to read back into the queer past right or wrong, utopian promise or sluggish moderation. Instead, they take the queer past—and, by extension, present—on its own terms. It is a similar

46

Magnus Hirschfeld was a pioneering sexologist and campaigner for homosexual rights in nineteenth- and twentieth-century Germany. Credited with founding the first homosexual rights movement in modern history, he has, in recent years, been criticized for his sometimes timid, assimilationist politics, for his complicity with empire, and for his use of racist language.

balancing act that we have had to attempt in recent years with our own flawed progressives, from Abraham Lincoln to FDR.

Indeed, to reject pragmatism would be to reject countless queer activist efforts from across the twentieth century. Many of the gay and lesbian liberation movements that started in the 1960s and 1970s had prominent pragmatic subcurrents, with activists who pressed for new legislation, secured funding for queer priorities, and endorsed policy changes that substantively improved the lives of queer people. These were activists, in short, who were willing to work with and within the state. At the same time, even the more radical branches of these movements were shot through with some of the same ambivalences as their more moderate counterparts. The West German gay and lesbian movement, for instance, was so riven by debates over socialism, gender, race, and the age of consent that it would be an impossible task to sort the competing factions into "radical" and "moderate" classes.[4] Likewise, the Gay Liberation Front that emerged in New York City after the 1969 Stonewall riots collapsed only a few years later, divided by questions of race, class, and gender.[5] To recover and understand these histories, scholars who take a more pragmatic approach to sexuality and the state have become adept at picking up on the inherent ambiguity of queerness past and present.

LGBTQ movements have often sought to work with states. Here, an American activist demands passage of a federal gay rights bill in 1978.

Likewise, when AIDS tore through queer communities in the United States, ACT UP did not just mobilize to halt the disease's spread in literal, photographable ways. As Sarah Schulman argues in *Let the Record Show*, a history of ACT UP New York, confronting the epidemic required an "Inside/Outside strategy" of both direct-action protests and policy experts who could persuade the government to confront the crisis.[6] In West Germany, queer activists allied with the center-right federal government to distribute information about the disease, blunting its spread. Many of the advances in LGBTQ rights have, in fact, come about thanks to collaboration with elements of the modern state. Such approaches necessitate viewing the state not as a monolithic whole— as radical approaches often do—but rather as a muddled assemblage of competing and conflicting parts that can be pressured, threatened, and cajoled into acting in the interests of the marginalized. Such a pragmatic approach queers the state in its embrace of messy ambiguity.

This pragmatism inflects much of the new historical scholarship on queerness. For instance, *Intimate States*, a 2021 collection of fourteen essays, examines the varied ways that elements of the American state, from municipal governments to federal courts, have historically regulated sex, gender, and sexuality. In doing so, the volume "captures the reality of state actions as emanating not from a stable entity—'the state'—but from a shifting pattern of governing powers."[7] In his exemplary contribution to the volume, trans legal scholar Paisley Currah focuses on contemporary regulations to highlight the inherent instability of the concept of the state. His essay underscores how, in New York City, "a woman could be housed in a women's homeless shelter, sent to a men's prison upstate, and have an F on her driver's license."[8] The different agencies arriving at these divergent sex classifications are all part of "the state," but each applies its own slightly different logics and procedures.

Questioning the homogeneity of "the state" allows us to make out its capriciousness as well as its capacity to achieve something that looks like progress. In this sense, it weds the critical impulses of queer theory to empirically grounded assessment. The three editors of *Intimate States* argue that the volume reveals how "protecting children as a route to securing the health of the social body led states to develop novel forms of knowledge as well as new ameliorative programs." At the same time, following more critical approaches, they emphasize that "state protection and access to public provision nonetheless came with surveillance and the potential for coercion," noting, for example, how New Deal programs encouraged the establishment of white, heterosexual families—progressive redistribution chained to racist patriarchy.[9] Because the volume's authors break the state apart into its constituent components—local and regional agencies,

51

legislators, courts—they can make out the good, the bad, and the mediocre in the relationship between queerness and the state.

To the extent that a politics or a theory of the state can be deduced from such scholarship, it is precisely the messy, pragmatic approach that has historically been the counterpart of more radical strands of queer thought. Where some see a monolithic whole, pragmatists see an agglomeration of competing interest groups and actors. Where some only see violence enacted against queer people, pragmatists make out both violence and opportunity. And where radical theorists believe in the sudden possibility of utopian promise, pragmatists argue, as Currah asserted in 2019, in conversation with queer legal scholar Aeyal Gross, "we can't just click our heels three times and bring a better state into existence."[10]

In that 2019 conversation, Gross and Currah began to sketch out what a queer theory of the state might look like. Currah suggested there is a place for activist efforts aimed at liberal recognition, but insisted, "I draw the line at arguments for inclusion that will have immediate negative effects on others,"[11] suggesting a liberal theory of least harm. Gross, whose scholarship focuses on queerness and international law, also echoed Currah's pragmatic approach, albeit slightly more skeptically. "Yes, the state has power and we often need it," Gross mused, "but we should also think beyond the state. This means turning to the state for recognition pragmatically, but without accepting that its policies constitute our relationships, or our lives."[12] Such a utilitarian approach to the state may be able to justify this or that policy, but it nevertheless leaves us trapped between the empirical need for the state and queer theory's inability to articulate why. Such a theory of the state is, in some sense, a theory of interest group activism in a democratic polity, inspired in part by the success of queer activists in the United States and Western Europe over the last seventy years. But it nonetheless fails to imagine that queers could ever be insiders within even a democratic system, that they might ever be the ones for whom that democratic state exists or who are represented through its sovereign organs.

While a pragmatic view of the state rebuts its radical rejection, it nonetheless fails to offer a positive vision of when, why, or how the various agencies, competencies, and sovereignties that compose the state can be useful to queers or can function in ways that align with the critical impulses of queer theory. Like modern liberalism, it must resign itself to holding two contradictory views at once: on the one hand, viewing the state as a source of violent oppression, while, on the other hand, acknowledging that only through the state can anything of substance be accomplished. In his afterword to *Intimate States*, historian Brent Cebul lands on precisely this formulation: that we need to rebuild the state from the ravages of neoliberalism, even if it is not entirely clear why or how we need it. He holds out hope, though, that we are living through "the beginnings of a truly emancipatory set of intimate rights in which the state plays a positive rather than discharging role."[13]

1   Laurie Marhoefer, *Sex and the Weimar Republic: German Homosexual Emancipation and the Rise of the Nazis* (Toronto: University of Toronto Press, 2015); Laurie Marhoefer, *Racism and the Making of Gay Rights: A Sexologist, His Student, and the Empire of Queer Love* (Toronto: University of Toronto Press, 2022); Heike Bauer, *The Hirschfeld Archives: Violence, Death, and Modern Queer Culture* (Philadelphia, PA: Temple University Press, 2017).
2   Javier Samper Vendrell, *The Seduction of Youth: Print Culture and Homosexual Rights in the Weimar Republic* (Toronto: University of Toronto Press, 2020).
3   Craig Griffiths, *The Ambivalence of Gay Liberation: Male Homosexual Politics in 1970s West Germany* (Oxford: Oxford University Press, 2021), 16–30.
4   Griffiths, *The Ambivalence of Gay Liberation*, 162–98.
5   Martin Duberman, *Has the Gay Movement Failed?* (Berkeley, CA: University of California Press, 2018), 3–49.
6   Sarah Schulman, *Let the Record Show: A Political History of ACT UP New York, 1987–1993* (New York: Farrar, Straus and Giroux, 2021), 86.
7   Margot Canaday, Nancy F. Cott, and Robert O. Self, "Introduction," in *Intimate States: Gender, Sexuality, and Governance in Modern US History*, ed. Margot Canaday, Nancy F. Cott, and Robert O. Self (Chicago: University of Chicago Press, 2021), 7.
8   Paisley Currah, "The Work That Sex Does," in *Intimate States*, 305. See also Paisley Currah, *Sex Is As Sex Does: Governing Transgender Identity* (New York: New York University Press, 2022).
9   Canaday et al., "Introduction," 7.
10  Joseph J. Fischel, "Social Justice for Gender and Sexual Minorities: A Discussion with Paisley Currah and Aeyal Gross," *Critical Analysis of Law* 6, no. 1 (2019): 88.
11  Fischel, "Social Justice," 94.
12  Fischel, "Social Justice," 100.
13  Brent Cebul, "Afterword: Frugal Governance, Family Values, and the Intimate Roots of Neoliberalism," in *Intimate States*, 335.

# IV
# A Queer State

"I think right now that Democratic leadership has a very large number of tools at their disposal. The president particularly. And it's really about time that we take the kid gloves off and start using them to govern."[1] In cold fury, Representative Alexandria Ocasio-Cortez responded thus to Senator Joe Manchin's decision to tank her party's mammoth Build Back Better bill in December 2021. Her words reflected a growing consensus among its progressive wing that state power—or certain forms of state power—is not something to be afraid of but rather something to be wielded.

To the extent that progressive politicians have begun to embrace the state again in recent years, the impetus has come largely from the activist left, spurred by groups like the Democratic Socialists of America and the

Working Families Party. Their reach, as well as their limits, are highlighted by Bernie Sanders's two failed presidential campaigns, the ascent of a new cohort of legislators, and the increasing willingness of the mainstream Democratic Party to entertain significant expansions of the welfare state. President Biden's administration in many ways captures the growing pains of this new, more muscular left. While the administration's vaunted Build Back Better program, pitched as a version of Representative Ocasio-Cortez's Green New Deal, failed to garner enough votes, thanks to Senator Manchin's opposition, a version infelicitously named the Inflation Reduction Act did pass in August 2022. Although the law was a mere fraction of what Biden had originally proposed, it represents the most robust climate legislation in the history of the United States.

But because these impulses have come out of the Marxian left—that is, from those who see class struggle as the driving force of politics—they have largely emerged in response to economic issues. And even then, only in fits and starts. The Biden administration's woefully equivocal response to economic insecurities reveals that its commitment to redistribution runs only an inch deep.

Moreover, when it comes to issues of identity and rights, it's clear that progressives struggle to articulate a coherent framework for thinking about the role of the state. Progressive politicians' response to the Supreme

Court's historic *Dobbs* decision striking down *Roe v. Wade* has, in the best cases, largely focused on supporting community abortion funds and ensuring that women in states that now ban abortion will be able to access the care they need. This is, of course, vital. But it can only be a bandage on the problem until there is a state that is able and willing to guarantee women's equal rights and access to care. Few politicians have yet endorsed any of the many creative solutions President Biden might adopt to counteract the Supreme Court's decision, from outright ignoring the Dobbs ruling or packing the Supreme Court to operating abortion clinics on federal lands or even calling a general strike. Democratic politicians' generally timid response to conservative courts' attempts to ban the abortifacient mifepristone in 2023 only confirms their unwillingness to govern. Even more concerning are recent polls, which suggest that fewer and fewer young Americans, who tend to skew progressive, view the state as a "meaningful" vehicle for change.[2]

Similarly, the party has remained disturbingly silent on the wave of transphobic and homophobic legislation sweeping across the country—the latest evidence that social conservatives have never shrunk from using the state to advance their agenda. A growing number of states, stoked by fascist "groomer" rhetoric, are passing laws banning transitioning among youth (and even adults) and censoring queer texts.[3] While they come, undoubtedly,

Spurred by fascist rhetoric equating drag, LGBTQ education, and gender-affirming care with sexual "grooming," far-right groups have taken to protesting queer events. Here, members of the paramilitary Proud Boys protest a drag queen story hour at the Queens Public Library in New York City.

from cynical attempts to turn out the Republican Party's shrinking core constituencies, it remains to be seen if they actually represent smart politics in a country that overwhelmingly approves of LGBTQ rights. Nonetheless, such measures and the increasingly violent rhetoric that accompanies them offer a terrifying vision of a future in which the extermination of queer people and cultures is state policy.

Both in the lead up to and after the 2022 elections, Democratic leaders preferred to tell their frustrated supporters that the best solution to any given national problem was to "vote," perhaps forgetting that the 2020 election had delivered to the party unified control of the federal government, that in fact they had the power to act. That forgetfulness is not, I think, strategic or even necessarily intentional; rather, it is the culmination of decades of neoliberal politicking and anti-statist theorizing, which have colluded to make Democrats unable to conceive positively of state power. As Walter Benjamin suggested of European parliamentarians a century ago, "they have not remained cognizant of the revolutionary forces to which they owe their existence."[4] Like the 1920s, this decade is shaping up to be a profoundly difficult moment for democracy and the liberal state. Liberal democracy is predicated, in practice if not in theory, on its ability to deliver the most good for the most people. But when it cannot accomplish this function—or, at least, when it can no longer persuade most of its citizens that it does—the state becomes suspect, first on the fringes of political life and then increasingly in the mainstream. What many centrist liberals (read: Democrats) don't seem to understand is that the status quo is no longer tenable. The center cannot hold. Liberal democracy is, in fact, a radical proposition, but as soon as we forget its radicalism and become content with a politics of maintenance, it starts to crumble. If we are to counter the rising threat of the populist right, something will have to give.

We might begin charting a new path by returning to Benjamin's critique of power, which resonates so deeply with queer critiques of the state. To directly compare the two, however, makes plain that something is missing in queer theory's approach. Its rejection of the state rests on the tacit assumption that force can be transcended, that with the right forms of critique and with the right kinds of direct action, we might loose history's moorings.

Yet Benjamin understood such hopes to be pure fantasy: there is no exterior to state power. When queer advocates call for a retreat from the state and a return to forms of community organizing as a way to escape the state's violence, they are engaged in wishful thinking. And if they imagine that there is any way to solve the crises we face without force, they are deluding themselves. "Every notion of a somehow conceivable solution to mortal tasks," Benjamin wrote, "remains impossible if power in all its forms is totally and principally excluded."[5] This is a point on which (some) liberals too can agree. Shklar put it bluntly: liberalism "does not dream of an end of public, coercive government." What it hopes to limit, instead, is "arbitrary, unexpected, unnecessary, and unlicensed" force.[6]

Power, by which Benjamin meant any relationship of force, is always connected to structures of legality—that is, to the state. And it varies in whether it sustains the existing order of things, destroys that order, or creates a new order. It is for this reason that a workers' strike, Benjamin wrote, is a form of power. By imagining a new order of things, it poses a challenge to the state. So too must the community organizing and direct action advocated by queer activists, if it is to pose a true challenge to the status quo, be understood as a form of power. Put slightly differently: it is impossible to break free of the power of the state. By challenging the state, we imagine an arrangement of force, a new kind of state, that itself represents power.

At the same time, the state, once it has been forced to accept a new order—whether by elections, strikes, or mass protests—prefers to legalize and thereby legitimize such exercises of power so that they become law-sustaining rather than a challenge to its own existence—a technique that Roderick Ferguson once named "the will to institutionality."[7] By co-opting, or even absorbing, challenges to its authority, the state negates their revolutionary potential. Much that poses as revolutionary resistance in our own time has, in fact, already been accounted for in the status quo's ledger of law-preserving power. Because the state has already accepted certain kinds or degrees of opposition, only truly unexpected or gargantuan protests will unsettle the order of things. Most protests instead actually serve the very state they appear to oppose by allowing it to function precisely as it expects and wishes to. Protest is, more often than not, an opportunity for the forces of order to reassert their supremacy.

In a Benjaminian reading, then, protest and critique can, at best, present a challenge to the state's power. At worst, they serve as unwitting props for the status quo. At no point can they ever challenge the necessity of power. What, then, is to be done?

Benjamin's solution to this problem is what he terms "divine" power. This is a "law-destroying" power that strikes without warning and is in essence fleeting, a kind of revolutionary force that annihilates order entirely.[8] It is, I think, similar to what philosopher Susan Buck-Morss has termed "moments of clarity"—flashes of moral inspiration that have the ability to overwhelm mendacity and self-interest and thereby change the course of history.[9] This is precisely what progressives must be able to accept: that, on the one hand, there is no way to escape either force or the state and, on the other hand, the need to harness such flashes of clarity that have the possibility to transcend the order of things. Thinking about the state in such a way would break free of a lifeless pragmatism that makes little room for inspiration, while also forcing radicals to acknowledge that power must be the end goal of protest and critique.

Some queer theorists have begun to think about politics in similar ways. Evren Savcı, a scholar of contemporary Turkey, recently identified queer theory's obsession with critique as part of a larger problem ailing the modern left. In a world disenchanted by the icy logics of neoliberalism, she writes, the deconstructionist impulse that forms the bedrock of queer theory "does not work to re-enchant the world."[10] Queerness-as-critique, that is, has ossified into ideology, alienating potential allies from broader queer struggles for economic, social, and political justice. Critique no longer performs the revolutionary function it once did.

In its place, Savcı imagines "a politics that centers feminist and queer joy," a politics that would not rest solely on critique but would rather draw its strength from "the re-enchanting promise of the commons."[11] Such a politics of joy would certainly not abandon critique but would instead privilege political alliances cutting across boundaries of class, gender, sexuality, and race. Any queer theory of the state would similarly have to make room for such a politics, to position itself as a project not just for a small caste of queer people with specific political goals, but rather as an overarching so-cial endeavor whose legitimacy derives from the mean-ing and joy it offers.

Hence, the state is, or ought to be, us, the commons, the people who live in the territory in which the state exerts its sovereignty. In an ideal world, this state might, perhaps, encompass the globe, for there have never been purer abuses of state power than those which occur in borderlands. The invocation that a state represent pop-ular sovereignty is, of course, an oversimplification of centuries of political thought, and one that risks ignor-ing the exclusionary ways in which that "us" has often been defined. Yet so much progressive thought, and especially queer thought, loses sight of the fact that the state is made up of and represents people, a messy multi-plicity of actors, as Currah points out, including "elected officials, political appointees, public servants" as well as voters, citizens, and subjects.[12] It ought not be contro-versial for us to accept that the state should represent our interests as faithfully as possible, even those interests we may not always know.[13]

A queer state would therefore be fundamentally demo-cratic. As we have seen, queer theory is often ambiva-lent on the question of democracy, largely because of queers' ambivalent experiences of democratic govern-ment. Yet any queer theory of the state would have to ac-cept a democratic outlook in order to escape the insidious traps of violence that queerness rejects. Democracy may be—in fact *is*—imperfect, but it is the queerest form of government yet invented. By institutionalizing the capacity for self-renewal through elections and freedom of expression, it is better able to take on critique than any other state form. It is the kind of government most capable of adjusting queerly, of self-reflexively adapting to the problems of the present.

Yet there is nothing to guide what version of democracy might best serve the needs of twenty-first-century progressivism. Democracy need not look like the current United States republic, which is, at best, only tenuously democratic. Rather, a queer democracy would focus not merely on democratic means—that is, on the pageantry of elections—but rather on what William Novak and Stephen Sawyer have termed, following John Dewey, "democratic ends," that is, policies that "equitably and effectively secured the people's actual health, safety, and well-being."[14] It must be based on a queer perspective, then, that takes materialism seriously and can distinguish between economic and social spheres, redistributing not merely recognition, but also material goods in the interest of the common weal. The problem, of course, is that a democratic majority may not always wish to pursue democratic ends and thus there is no easy way of defining what a "democratic end" might be or how a polity might achieve it.

So, what might it look like? To start with, queer democracy would break with the long tradition of liberal monadism. It would not take the sovereign independence of the individual as its starting point but would instead acknowledge the existence of that "us," the communitarian foundation of the state and of society. Moreover, it would be an "us" that takes imbricated forms of difference seriously, while rejecting the worn-out opposition of class and identity.[15] As we have seen, queer theory questions the very concept of the individual, revealing how we are all enmeshed in systems of normative power that shape our choices and life opportunities, even if we believe ourselves possessed of agency. "We are social," Butler contends in an essay on the politics of mourning, "we are comported toward a 'you'; we are outside ourselves, constituted in cultural norms that precede and exceed us, given over to a set of cultural norms and a field of power that condition us fundamentally."[16] The point, as I see it, is not that we are without agency, but rather that it is the very myth of agency constituted in a liberal political paradigm that deprives us of it. Our agency can only ever take on meaning through collective action. True democracy can only ever be communitarian in its outlook, for by believing that we have agency as individuals we are robbed of it.

Through collective action, then, comes what Bonnie Honig calls "public things"—"a national park system, public cemeteries, public education, and more." These are the commons that breathe life into the bare institutions of democratic governance. "Procedures, polling, and policing," Honig tells us, are "all necessary, perhaps, but certainly not sufficient conditions of democratic life."[17] But if we have democratic ends in the stuff of public things, we do not yet have the means to attain or to preserve them. It is rather in the imagined public of this re-enchanted commons that we might find such means. Democracy thus springs from the joyful proposition that we do have obligations to each other in this life and—crucially—that it is within our power to fulfill them.

Yet, we cannot simply will away those who wish us ill. And so, a queer state, while founded on muscular democratic principles, would also welcome the possibility for robust criticism that both prevents mythologies of the state from taking shape and leaves open the possibility of sudden, emancipatory change. It must be a state that accepts the never-ending possibility of its own demise. But like the propagation of a giant sequoia, whose cones have adapted to release their seeds in the dry heat of a forest fire, such a demise would not be one of destruction, but of rebirth. A queer theory of the state would necessitate that queer theory, and progressive politics more broadly, leave behind its anti-majoritarian impulses and its fear of state power while retaining its potent faculties of critique. It would have to imagine a power without norms, an honest power that declares itself as such and acknowledges its own mutability, but a power that is willing to impose its decisions.

A queer way of being in and of the state, then, would have to give up queer theory's fetish for marginalization—what Heather Love has criticized as its "normative injunction to be deviant."[18] Doing so would resolve one paradox at the heart of the queer project, namely that for all of the field's anti-normative impulses, its practitioners do, in fact, typically harbor normative agendas for which they advocate.[19] Acknowledging this to be the case—accepting that queer theory can, in fact, make normative claims—would not only rid it of this Foucauldian hangover but would also clear a major obstacle to its ability to envision a queer state.

A queer state would thus enable critique, but it would be critique with purpose, not the kind of points-scoring criticism that today can seem woefully common on the left. Put another way, it must be critique that can distinguish between strategy and theory—that can, as Lisa Duggan pointed out decades ago, mobilize its critical insights for the purposes of winning elections and advancing policy.[20]

Let us return, for a moment, to where we began: the mpox scare of 2022. The episode revealed something profound about queerness in the United States, a yawning divide between those who are primarily motivated by critique and those who are loath to let the perfect be the enemy of the good, but who too willingly accept the imperfect status quo. Both sides have their points. But in April 2023, months after the administration had declared an end to the health emergency, the queer essayist Joseph Osmundson shared new data showing that 90 percent of those who died from the disease were Black men; 95 percent had untreated HIV. His point was that while mpox may have been a solvable inconvenience for privileged, white queers, it was a crisis for Black Americans without access to healthcare. "If you think MPOX is over," he tweeted, "ask yourself FOR WHOM?"[21]

With the benefit of (a degree of) hindsight, I have started to think of the country's response to the disease as an encapsulation of what a queer state might look like. The US government did respond to the threat—belatedly, timidly, halfheartedly, yes, but it did. Queer activists mobilized to demand better of the state and the government responded: it ramped up vaccine distribution, it made efforts to reach underserved and underprivileged communities, and it has virtually eliminated the disease in this country.[22] That is to say, queer activists engaged in a kind of constructive critique that recognizes the need for coordinated state action. My point is not to excuse the tepid response of the government in the moment, but rather to point to the mobilization of activists as an example of the kind of non-cynical critique that would need to become the norm in any queer state.

There is a mural not far from my home titled *Together*, which was completed in 2021. It celebrates the energy of the 2017 Women's March on Washington, one of the largest protests in American history that set the stage for the democratic revival through which I hope we are currently living (see p. 13). This joyful work of art depicts thousands of people, multihued, coming together to form the capitol dome, the very sign and seal of our popular sovereignty. It is an image of community and warmth, which starts to get at what queer democracy might feel like. For whatever we term it—whether Benjamin's divine power, Buck-Morss's moments of clarity, or Savcı's re-enchanted commons—a queer theory of the state would have to self-critically, joyfully embrace that democratic "us" which sits at the root of sovereignty. The trouble in envisioning exactly what such a state might look like lies precisely in the evanescent nature of queerness: because it is constantly changing, constantly critiquing, constantly in flux, one cannot imagine it pausing long enough to, say, write a constitution. And so, a queer theory of the state is never likely to be worked out in enough formal detail to constitute an actually existing state, but rather remains, at best, a set of principles and hopes through which we queers (by which I hope to mean every human on Earth) might approach the tasks of statehood. A queer state, to put it simply, would never be a finished product; it would never reach utopia. Rather, it would see in itself a constant, asymptotic striving to betterment on behalf of all citizens, indeed all life, even beyond humanity. A queer way of being *in* and *of* the state would mean nothing less than democracy, both utopian and pragmatic, ever hopeful in its eagerness to improve and clear-eyed in its acceptance of that which lies beyond the reach of power.

1   Alexandria Ocasio-Cortez, "Morning Joe," MSNBC, December 20, 2021.
2   Myah Ward, "Young Voters Are Getting Less Likely to Identify as Dems," *Politico*, July 17, 2023, https://www.politico.com/news/2023/07/13/biden-2024-election-young-voters-00106262.
3   Samuel Clowes Huneke, "Dangerous as the Plague," *The Baffler*, June 23, 2022, https://thebaffler.com/latest/dangerous-as-the-plague-huneke.
4   Walter Benjamin, "Zur Kritik der Gewalt," in *Walter Benjamin, Gesammelte Schriften*, vol. II–I, ed. Rolf Tiedemann and Hermann Schweppenhäuser (Frankfurt: Suhrkamp, 1977), 190.
5   Benjamin, "Zur Kritik der Gewalt," 196.
6   Shklar, "The Liberalism of Fear," 29.
7   Roderick Ferguson, "Administering Sexuality; or, the Will to Institutionality," *Radical History Review* 100 (Winter 2008): 163.
8   Benjamin, "Zur Kritik der Gewalt," 199.
9   Susan Buck-Morss, *Hegel, Haiti, and Universal History* (Pittsburgh: University of Pittsburgh Press, 2009), 75.
10  Evren Savcı, *Queer in Translation: Sexual Politics under Neoliberal Islam* (Durham, NC: Duke University Press, 2021), 111.
11  Savcı, *Queer in Translation*, 122, 111.
12  Paisley Currah, "The State," *Transgender Studies Quarterly* 1, nos. 1–2 (2014): 198.
13  As Jean-Jacques Rousseau memorably put it, "Whoever refuses to obey the general will shall be constrained to do so by the whole body, which means nothing other than that he shall be forced to be free." Jean-Jacques Rousseau, *The Social Contract*, trans. Maurice Cranston (London: Penguin, 1968), 64.

14  Novak and Sawyer, "Epilogue," 113; Pierre Rosanvallon, *Democracy Past and Future*, ed. Samuel Moyn (New York: Columbia University Press, 2006), 196–97; Brown, *Undoing the Demos*, 210.

15  Lisa Duggan, "Reimagining the State," *WSQ: Women's Studies Quarterly* 51, nos. 1–2 (Spring/Summer 2023): 243–48.

16  Judith Butler, *Precarious Life: The Powers of Mourning and Violence* (London: Verso, 2006), 45.

17  Bonnie Honig, *Public Things: Democracy in Disrepair* (New York: Fordham University Press, 2017), 4.

18  Love, *Underdogs*, 37.

19  Paisley Currah, "Homonationalism, State Rationalities, and Sex Contradictions," *Theory & Event* 16, no. 1 (2013).

20  Lisa Duggan, "Queering the State," *Social Text* 39 (Summer 1994): 8–9.

21  Joseph Osmundson, Twitter, April 14, 2023, 11:31 a.m., https://twitter.com/reluctantlyjoe/status/1646898955228262406?s=20.

22  "U.S. Mpox Case Trends Reported to CDC," Centers for Disease Control and Prevention, updated April 12, 2023, https://www.cdc.gov/poxvirus/mpox/response/2022/mpx-trends.html.

# Acknowledgments

A version of this essay was first published as "Toward a Queer Theory of the State" in *The Point* on July 26, 2022.

My sincere thanks to my editors at *The Point*, Jon Baskin and Julia Aizuss, who helped to shape the original piece. Thanks also to Aaron Bogart, who encouraged me to expand this research into the essay you have before you, and to Sam Lebovic, Roger Pellegrini, and Nathaniel Edwards, who read earlier drafts and made many helpful suggestions along the way. Finally, my gratitude to Evren Savcı, who read the manuscript in its final stages and offered generous, incisive critiques that substantially improved the ultimate copy.

# Biography

Samuel Clowes Huneke is assistant professor of history at George Mason University. His first book, *States of Liberation: Gay Men Between Dictatorship and Democracy in Cold War Germany* (2022), won the Charles E. Smith Award for best book in European History from the Southern Historical Association. Huneke has written for *Boston Review*, *The Washinton Post*, *The Point*, and the *Los Angeles Review of Books*.

# Image Credits

P. 13
Thousands attend Women's March on Washington, DC, 2017; © Getty Images; Photo: Aaron P. Bernstein

P. 16
Demonstration held in NYC calling on more government action to combat spread of monkeypox; © Getty Images; Photo: Jeenah Moon

P. 17
ACT UP demonstrates for an AIDS cure at the 25th Gay Parade; © Getty Images; Photo: Allan Tannenbaum

P. 24
David Robinson, ACT UP founding member and Ashes Action organizer, Washington, DC, 1992; Courtesy of the photographer; Photo: Megan Handler

P. 31
The Government Has Blood on Its Hands. One AIDS Death Every Half Hour, 1988. Courtesy of Gran Fury; image from the public domain, www.granfury.org

P. 40
Martin Dannecker at Germany's first gay march forty-five years ago; © Picture Alliance/dpa/Archiv Rosa Geschichten Münster

P. 49
Gay rights banner; © Getty Images; Photo: Peter Keegan

P. 47
Magnus Hirschfeld, 1928; © *Sueddeutsche Zeitung*/Alamy Stock Photos

P. 58
US rights drag protest; © Getty Images; Photo: Yuki Iwamura

Every effort has been made to trace the copyright holders and obtain permission to reproduce this material. The publisher apologizes for any errors or omissions in the above list and would be grateful if notified of any corrections that should be incorporated in future reprints or editions of this book.

# Colophon

Series editor:
Aaron Bogart

Copyediting:
Louisa Elderton

Editorial assistance:
Jude Macannuco

Graphic design:
Daniela Burger

Typesetting:
Vreni Knödler

Typeface:
Kelvin Avec Clair

Printing:
druckhaus köthen

Paper:
F-color Karton Feinkorn,
Munken Print White

Published by
Floating Opera Press
Hasenheide 9
10967 Berlin
www.floatingoperapress.com

ISBN 978-3-9823894-6-2

Printed in Germany